W9-ALX-966

MAKING A BETTER WRLD

# Recycling

141367

## By Gary Chandler and Kevin Graham

**Twenty-First Century Books**

A Division of Henry Holt and Company
New York

Twenty-First Century Books
A division of Henry Holt and Company, Inc.
115 West 18th Street
New York, New York 10011

Henry Holt® and colophon are registered trademarks of
Henry Holt and Company, Inc.
*Publishers since 1866*

©1996 by Blackbirch Graphics, Inc.
First Edition
5 4 3 2 1
All rights reserved.
No part of this book may be reproduced in any form without permission
in writing from the publisher, except by a reviewer.

Published in Canada by Fitzhenry & Whiteside Ltd.
195 Allstate Parkway, Markham, Ontario L3R 4T8

Printed in the United States of America on acid free paper.

Created and produced in association with Blackbirch Graphics, Inc.
*Series Editor:* Tanya Lee Stone

**Library of Congress Cataloging-in-Publication Data**

Chandler, Gary.
 Recycling / by Gary Chandler and Kevin Graham.
  p.    cm. — (Making a better world)
 Includes index.
 Summary: Presents an overview of recycling processes and describes how recycled plastic, paper, fibers, and other materials can be used to create all kinds of new
products.
 ISBN 0-8050-4622-4
 1. Recycling (Waste, etc.)—Juvenile literature. 2. Recycled products—Juvenile
literature. [1. Recycling (Waste). 2. Recycled products.] I. Graham, Kevin.
II. Title. III. Series: Making a better world (New York, N.Y.)
TD794.5.C46  1996
363.72'82—dc20                                                96-23068
                                                                CIP
                                                                AC

# Table of Contents

# Welcome to
# Making a Better World

Recycling is just one piece of the environmental puzzle, but it's an area where everyone can get involved. Recycling involves re-using household and industrial materials, such as plastic and paper products. It not only helps to cut waste, but also reduces our use of resources and lessens the pollution that results from processing those resources. New laws have required recycling in more and more areas. Companies are designing products more efficiently and from materials that are either made of recycled materials or that can be recycled. Corporations and large organizations are recycling to save money on garbage disposal fees. Other organizations and individuals are recycling various items, such as soda bottles, as a method of raising money. Many do so simply because they know recycling is healthy for the environment.

As a result of all this new activity, recycling rates in the United States and elsewhere around the world have reached record levels. As more uses develop for recycled materials, the demand will boost the prices for these products and recycling rates should keep growing. This book will introduce you to a number of new and innovative examples of recycling being used today.

All of the books in *Making a Better World* report on people—kids, parents, schools, neighborhoods, and companies—who have decided to get involved in a cause they believe in.  Through their dedication, commitment, and dreams, they helped to make ours a better world.  Each one of the stories in this book will take you through the steps of what it took for some ordinary people to achieve something extraordinary. Of course, in the space of one book, we can share only a fraction of the wonderful stories that exist. After a long and complicated selection process, we have chosen what we believe are the most exciting subjects to tell you about.

We hope this book will encourage you to learn more about recycling. Better yet, we hope all the books in this series inspire you to get involved. There are plenty of ways that each individual—including you—can make a better world. You will find some opportunities throughout this book—and there are many others out there waiting for you to discover. If you would like to write to us for more information, the address is Earth News, P.O. Box 101413, Denver, CO 80250.

Sincerely,

Gary Chandler
and
Kevin Graham

# Recycling Plastic

Recycling plastic saves energy, money, and precious landfill space. New uses for recycled plastic are gaining in popularity. In order to keep the recycled plastic industry growing, collection systems for plastic bottles and containers are being developed across the United States. As time goes on, hopefully a national system will be put in place.

Today, the demand for recycled plastic greatly exceeds the supply. Better product design and increased public awareness about proper packaging will improve the efficient use and reuse of plastic. In 1995, polyethylene terephthalate (PET) bottle recycling in the United States reached a record high at 34 percent of the bottles produced. Despite the success, this statistic means that 66 percent still ended up in landfills. This shows that there is still a lot of room for improved environmental education and awareness on the part of the general public.

## From Bottles to Benches

Turning the fruits of a recycling program into usable results has proven particularly successful for the Chicago, Illinois, Park District and the city's residents. As a result of their efforts, Chicago's 563 parks are now filled with garbage—but this is good! The garbage is in the form of benches, playground barriers, and other items composed completely of plastic that has been donated by residents in the city's Plastic On Parks (POP) program.

At the beginning of the project, 400 pounds of plastic were collected each week. Eventually, that number increased by 100 times, to more than 40,000 pounds of plastic each week. "When you contribute to a project and can see what your efforts are creating, it's a lot easier to get excited about it," says Leonard Lauricella, assistant director of landscape management for the park district. "Local citizens know their plastic bottles are becoming useful items." The program got a shot in the arm thanks to a public service announcement featuring professional basketball player Michael Jordan. "Recycle With Michael" was the theme of the promotion.

Under the program, residents brought their empty plastic milk, water, and soda pop containers to their local city recreation centers. Because of the volume, the park district dedicated a truck solely to collecting the bottles, and it had to stop at some of the centers every day. The bottles were then sorted and shipped to Plastic Recycling, Inc., in Iowa Falls, Iowa. This company creates plastic "lumber." After processing the plastic, the product is sent back to Chicago. "Our contract required the company to return the same plastic we gave them," Lauricella explains. "This is why people do it—they can see what is being done with the plastic."

Most of the "plastic wood" has been used to refurbish hundreds of the city's playgrounds. Approximately 350,000 plastic bottles are needed per playground. A 12-inch-high perimeter wall is built around each playground using the lumber, and the inner area is then filled with a soft material that feels like wood chips or sand. The unique lumber also has been used to build park benches and floating docks. "Our carpenters have no problem with the plastic," Lauricella says. "It cuts like wood, saws like wood, and nails like wood." But the plastic lumber doesn't deteriorate like wood, and children don't have to worry about splinters. Also, the plastic is graffiti-resistant because it is nonporous and can easily be cleaned.

*In 1991, the Chicago Park District and the Chicago Cubs baseball club joined together to promote the recycling of plastics.*

"We've collected more than 2 million pounds of plastic since we started," Lauricella notes. "If we've diverted that much material from landfills, then we've helped to lengthen the lives of those landfills and benefited everyone here."

Chicago's Park District discontinued the POP program in 1993 after it finished rebuilding its playgrounds. The park district has received many inquiries from other cities regarding the POP program and has offered to lend whatever assistance it can to help establish similar recycling programs in other communities.

*Recycled plastic was used in the form of "lumber" to build the low wall of this playground.*

## For More Information

*To start a similar program, write to Plastic Recycling, Inc., 10252 Highway 65, Iowa Falls, IA 50126-8823, or call (515) 648-5073.*

# *Turning Plastic Bottles into Fences*

One company is finding profitable new ways to use recycled plastic by building woodlike fences and decks out of ground-up plastic bottles. Calling its product "the last fence you'll ever build," a Denver, Colorado, company is turning plastic milk bottles into some of the longest-lasting fences around. The bottles for the fencing material are bought after they have already been ground into pellet form. Any drink or bleach bottle made with a type of plastic called HDPE can be used in the fencing. The final product, called Plasti-Fence, is made of 100 percent recycled materials.

After they are collected, the bottles are sorted, stripped of labels, and ground into small chips. They are then washed and dried. Initial production of the fencing started in late 1992, when a six-foot-high, typical privacy fence was test-marketed in the Denver area through a chain of home-center stores. The product sold well.

This unique fence is produced with a simulated wood grain in either a cedar, brown, or country-white color. The product comes with a 20-year limited warranty—better than any wood products because it won't rot or splinter. It can be sawed, screwed, or bolted like wood, and it is virtually dirt-, stain-, and graffiti-proof because most marks won't adhere permanently to HDPE plastic.

"A 100-foot section of our fence keeps 5,000 one-gallon plastic containers out of landfills," boasts Gene Pendry, president and founder of Recycled Plastic Products, Inc. "And no

trees need to be cut down to make it, either." The Plasti-Fence comes with recycled plastic posts, rails, and pickets to make a complete fence. In addition, Plasti-Fence plans to introduce plastic lumber for decking and recycled plastic tire stops for parking lots.

*Gene Pendry and sales manager Bob Williams swim in plastic bottles that will be made into Plasti-Fence.*

### For More Information

*Write to Plasti-Fence, 2331 W. Hampden Avenue, Suite 148, Englewood, CO 80110, or call (800) 235–7940.*

# Converting Pop Bottles into Homes

Another company has been working to find innovative uses for recycled plastic. ThermaLock has developed a new building block—partially composed of recycled plastic—that can take the place of normal concrete blocks in construction projects and create energy-efficient buildings.

While the ThermaLock Block is similar to the concrete block used in many buildings, this product consists of a thick layer of molded plastic sandwiched between two layers of concrete. When the blocks are cemented together, the new wall takes shape with an extra layer of continuous insulation, due to the plastic layer inside. This layer contains up to 30 percent recycled plastic and is designed to make walls five times more resistant to heat loss than other building blocks.

"The primary purpose of the ThermaLock Block is to save energy," explains Ken Blake, co-founder of ThermaLock. "But we're also showing how we can bury plastic waste in walls instead of in landfills." Currently, regulations for building blocks limit the maximum amount of recycled plastic that can be used to 30 percent. Blake hopes the regulations in America change fast enough to start using 50 percent recycled plastic in his product soon.

The idea caught the attention of *R&D* magazine. In 1993, the publication honored the new product as one of its "R&D 100"—an annual award for the most significant research and development efforts in the world.

# What Is a Landfill?

One major benefit of recycling is the reduction of trash. Millions of tons of trash are dumped into landfills—large holes in the ground—every day. Some are specifically dug to hold garbage, while others are converted from rock quarries or mines. In some cases, they are small canyons and ravines. New landfills are more environmentally sound than old ones, since they are lined at the bottom with plastic or dense soil to prevent water from leaking through the waste and then into groundwater supplies. Because many landfills often have not had this layer of protection, groundwater has been polluted with "leachate"—contaminated water.

Every American generates about a half ton of garbage each year, and it doesn't take long for even the largest landfills to reach capacity. Once full, most landfills are covered with dirt and leveled off so that water runs off them. Replacing these landfills has become more difficult than in the past due to health and environmental concerns, rising land costs, and the higher fuel costs necessary to reach new dumps. By reducing the amount of garbage through recycling, we can make these dumps last longer and lessen the need for new ones.

As the garbage in a landfill breaks down over time, it creates methane and sulfurous gases, which smell like rotten eggs. In addition to having an unpleasant odor, these gases are extremely explosive. Newer landfill facilities and some old ones have been tapped with pipes that allow the gases to escape. In some cases, the gases can even be burned to generate electricity.

To learn more about how landfills operate, you can take a "video fieldtrip." This gives you an inside look at the processes used to handle your trash. A videotape called "Garbage Day" is available at many public libraries. (This program won an award in 1994.) You can also write to ChildVision Educational Films, P.O. Box 2587, Los Angeles, CA 90078, or call (213) 463-3165, to purchase a copy of "Garbage Day."

# Recycling Paper

*P*aper makes up the largest portion of America's solid waste. In 1993, about 73 million *tons* of newspaper and paper were disposed of in the United States! Fortunately, about 40 percent of this vast quantity of paper was recovered and recycled. The majority of paper production relies on trees for pulp fiber, so recycling can save forests and landfill space. In order to improve the efficiency of paper recycling, however, better collection systems and better sorting methods are needed. Meanwhile, inadequate public education and awareness are also barriers to paper-recycling efficiency. Everyone needs to understand the importance of recycling paper and the proper procedures for doing it effectively.

# Turning Old Maps into New Envelopes

While recycling paper reduces long-term harm to the environment, simply re-using paper helps because it avoids the repulping process. One product made with re-used paper is MAPelopes—colorful, exotic envelopes made directly from surplus and outdated maps. The envelopes spare trees and landfills, as well as the chemicals and water needed to produce recycled paper.

Enzo and Matthew Magnozzi, founders of Forest Saver Inc., which deals in recycled-paper stationery products, came across the idea by accident. While placing an order to have envelopes made, Enzo threw in some old maps a friend had given him. He wanted the white side of the maps to form the outside of the envelopes, but the envelope maker misunderstood and did the opposite.

"People just love it," Enzo says. "It evolved out of a mistake and is now our major product. We're selling five tons' worth of old maps every month, and these products are even better than recycled paper because they are being re-used instead of recycled. It takes energy to produce recycled paper. The maps are ready to go—it's simply second use."

The map idea has evolved into other product lines as well, such as writing sets and notepads. When a map is reproduced so that it looks light or faded, some people like writing directly on the map side. Others prefer the white or back side of the products. And map lovers enjoy trying to figure out what part of the world a MAPelope represents.

*Forest Saver Inc. turns old maps into colorful and unique stationery.*

Forest Saver's main suppliers of maps have been map manufacturers and map distributors. Initially, they provided a free supply of outdated topographical maps. Because of the success of the idea, however, the company now must purchase the maps. Forest Saver's MAPelopes alone divert 60 tons of paper from landfills every year.

Enzo Magnozzi's personal favorites are MAPelopes made from maps of coastal areas with cities mixed in. He's also fond of the Great Salt Lake maps, and he enjoyed making products out of obsolete world maps after the Soviet Union disintegrated several years ago. "But there are so many nice ones, it's hard to choose. The color schemes on different maps can be great." He adds, "The products are not only interesting but also good for the environment."

## For More Information

*Write to MAPelopes/Forest Saver, 1860 Pond Road, Ronkonkoma, NY 11779, or call (800) 777–9886.*

# The "Wood" of the Future

What started as an idea for a sixth grader's science project is now a building material that looks like polished granite, but it can be cut and fastened with typical woodworking tools.

In 1991, a Minnesota student mixed old newspapers and Elmer's glue together in a blender, then used a microwave to harden the material. Several scientists from nearby Mankato State University were so impressed with the material that they soon formed a company—with the student involved—to perfect the formula and test market the new product.

"We've created a product similar to fiberglass," explains Lenny Jass, the president of the company, Phenix Biocomposites. "There are resins to hold the mixture together and fibers to add strength. Our material uses soybean flour as the resin and shredded recycled newspapers for its fibers."

The new material is called Environ, and it comes in a variety of colors and textures. To produce 18 square feet of the product—about the size of a large desktop—approximately 55 pounds of old newspapers and one bushel of soybeans are required. Three patents are pending on various processes and mixtures used in making Environ.

"We think of Environ as a new generation of hardwood," Jass says. "As with oak, you can use Environ in furniture, cabinets, wall systems, moldings, picture frames, and in plenty of other ways." To that end, Phenix Biocomposite's initial marketing efforts have centered on manufacturers of furniture, desks, and countertops.

*17*

*Opposite: Old newspaper and soybeans are processed to make a strong building material called Environ. Left: The finished Environ product looks like polished granite but uses recycled materials.*

"We not only help the environment by pulling newspapers out of the waste stream, but we're also using soybean flour—an underutilized by-product of soybean-oil manufacturing," Jass notes. "And unlike similar board products, we do not use harmful chemicals like formaldehyde during the production of Environ."

The product is also safer to use than comparable plastic-based products. Breathing in dust from some of those other products can be dangerous, but working with Environ is like working with wood. "To manufacture Environ, we deal with nothing unusual," he says. "No masks, no fumes—nothing strange to protect our workers from. All of the chemistry involved is water-based."

The company is starting to get the recognition it deserves. *Building Products*, a quarterly magazine that covers the building-products industry, named Phenix Biocomposites one of its five "green giants" in 1994. This means that it considers Phenix Biocomposites one of the most environmentally responsible companies in the industry.

## For More Information

*Write to Phenix Biocomposites, P.O. Box 609, Mankato, MN 56002-0609, or call (800) 324–8187.*

# Country's Oldest Paper Recycler Faces Challenges

Anyone who thinks that recycled paper is something new should talk to a New Hampshire company that has made recycled paper from 100 percent post-consumer waste since 1883.

Paper Services Limited is America's oldest producer of paper from recycled materials. It started making paper from cotton, silk, and linen rags more than 100 years ago to produce silk tissue paper used as packaging for garments.

Today, the mill accepts a wide variety of paper for recycling, including some materials that other recyclers will not accept. Sources for Paper Services' products include newspapers, glossy inserts, copy paper, old money, unbound books, stitched magazines, fax paper, and some junk mail.

"We used four million pounds of trash to make three million pounds of paper in 1994," says Gary O'Neal, the company's chief executive officer, "and that's with our mill operating at just 20 percent of capacity."

Unfortunately, the market has been tough for this struggling mill. Many of the same entities—cities such as Boston, Cambridge, and New Haven—that sell waste paper to the mill won't buy it back after recycling.

"Our clients want us to help them recycle their waste paper, but they won't buy back the recycled end products," O'Neal explains. "They aren't closing the recycling loop."

Another painful contradiction came from New York State. Paper Services was the first company allowed to use the state's "New Generation" emblem, created for recycled products of

*Old newspaper is recycled into new paper products by Paper Services Limited.*

high merit. The state, however, refuses to buy O'Neal's recycled products because they are slightly more expensive than products made from previously unused materials.

High energy costs in New Hampshire and the rising cost of waste paper also pose problems for Paper Services. The company has received numerous offers to relocate the mill to areas with lower operating costs, but O'Neal feels too much loyalty to the community to move to a more competitive location.

*Gary O'Neal explains the process of making paper to schoolchildren.*

Helping the community restore the local river is the company's greatest success. The company voluntarily built its own wastewater treatment facility in 1970 to help save the river. "The Ashuelot River is cleaner today than it was 100 years ago," O'Neal explains. "We don't take from the river—we borrow from it and return the water cleaner than when we diverted it." As a result of the company's concern and support, the Ashuelot River was recently placed in the New Hampshire Rivers Management and Protection Program. In 1995, the Environmental Protection Agency named the mill as a national model for recycling.

### For More Information

*Write to Paper Services Limited, Box 45, Hinsdale, NH 03451, or call (603) 239–6344.*

# Cows Browse Through
# the Yellow Pages

A herd of cows in Maine is letting its hooves do the walking through the Yellow Pages in one of the more unique uses of obsolete telephone books. More than five tons of old phone directories are shredded up every week and used as cow bedding on Ronald Webb's dairy farm. To get Webb started, several tons of phone books were delivered free of charge to the farm by NYNEX Information Resources Company, the publisher of NYNEX telephone directories in the area.

The phone books are used instead of sawdust or hay, creating less dust and better traction for the cows, and preventing them from slipping in the barn. "The material has good absorption qualities," says Ted Brown of Hannaford Brothers, a company involved in the project. "Mr. Webb has not lost a cow to slippage since the project started two years ago. Usually, an average of two cows a year are lost when they slip and break a pelvis or leg."

"The paper is more absorbent and creates a drier and cleaner bedding," says David Jean of NYNEX. "The key reason for participating in this study was to develop an alternative to landfilling a portion of municipal solid waste by composting the organic component of the solid waste stream." An unforeseen benefit from these improved conditions in the barn was a large reduction in udder infections, and thus a greater yield and higher quality of milk. Testing determined that ink from the shredded phone books has no adverse affect on the cows.

*23*

Once the cows have used the phone books, the soiled bedding from the Webb farm is composted with organic waste and used as fertilizer.

Once the bedding is soiled and replaced with a new batch of shredded phone books, the old bedding is mixed with food scraps and composted. Because only organic material is used, the dairy farmer is able to simply add it to the soiled bedding. The composted material is then used on the farm's fields. Testing also showed that the ink from the Yellow Pages had no negative effect on the soil that took the compost.

Woods End Research Laboratory in Maine provided the recipe for the bedding mixture and conducted all the testing. Woods End is an international leader of composting. Hannaford Brothers, a local grocery-store chain, assists Webb in the composting project by supplying him with organic food waste. Hannaford Brothers supplies roughly two tons of food scraps a week. The waste is composed of trimmings from produce and unsaleable products.

"This is a local effort that is providing a solution," says Brown. "Our interest is high because this does good things for the grocery industry. It takes about 40 percent of our waste stream and gets it back into the ground naturally."

# Recycling Computer Equipment

*T*he computer world is fast-paced and ever-changing. New ideas and technology are constantly prompting the development of products. New ones seem to show up nearly every day. Thus, by the time that an average consumer or corporation learns how to use a new computer system or software package, it is often already outdated. Needless to say, this trend creates lots of trash.

Fortunately, new ideas are now providing various recycling avenues for much of the equipment used in the computer world. These ideas are allowing older equipment to be re-used instead of being hauled to landfills where they may spend eternity underground.

# Computing Away Trash

With respect to the computer world, the conservation age has met the information age, and new ideas are transforming many waste problems into social and economic opportunities. In 1991, for instance, Californian Mark Hass cleared out a warehouse filled with old computers. First he tried to give them away. On such short notice, however, he was unsuccessful and ended up dumping them all.

That experience sparked an idea that has grown into a non-profit corporation called the Computer Recycling Center. Hass, along with Steven Wyatt and Will Marshman, founded the organization in 1992 after discovering that many companies were happy to give away their old computers and schools were equally happy to accept them. "The idea got an excellent reception," Hass recalls. "It was clear from the beginning that companies had a problem getting rid of their old computers."

With both collection and distribution systems now in place, the Computer Recycling Center takes in thousands of old computers and parts a month at its main facility in Mountain View, California, as well as at two other northern California locations. Huge trucks loaded with used computer equipment arrive every week from such companies as IBM, the Bank of California, and National Semiconductor.

A staff of hundreds of volunteers then tears into the donated machines, readying them for use in public schools. The volunteers clean the computers and perform diagnostic tests of various operating systems. Broken machines are used for their parts. In addition, Geoworks Corporation, a computer software firm, allows the center to place a working copy of its

Geoworks Pro software on every donated computer. The software features excellent graphics and runs on older computers, giving them new and useful lives.

Because the center does not pay shipping fees, schools arrange for shipping or come to the distribution facilities to pick up computers for their classrooms. The Computer Recycling Center requires that computers must be for public education and must be part of tax-exempt, non-religious organizations. The center has placed tens of thousands of computers, printers,

*The Computer Recycling Center rescues old computers and gives them new life.*

27

Property of
Bayport-Blue Point Public Library

*Older or broken computers are recycled for use by children in public schools.*

monitors, sealed software packages, and other peripherals in California schools and nonprofit organizations. "We're now in the process of replicating our operation—helping get other centers started," Wyatt explains. "We have state officials, city managers, community leaders, and entrepreneurs from across the country visiting us and requesting our help in setting up local and regional centers elsewhere."

Without suitable outlets, more than six billion pounds of computer hardware will end up in landfills over the next ten years. There are an estimated 60 million personal computers currently operating in the United States, each with an average useful life of five years. "In every major city, each of those big buildings has a computer sitting on every desk—and all companies periodically upgrade them and have to do something with the old computers," he explains. "We're setting up an avenue to create a flow of computers to schools. It's good for the community, businesses, and the environment." Not only does the center recycle and re-use computer equipment, but it also provides equipment that other segments of society find very useful. And even though the computers may someday end up in a landfill, the more things are re-used, the less new products need to be processed.

In addition to its computer-recycling efforts, the center is a state-licensed, post-secondary vocational training school. "We've developed a variety of courses involving hardware, software, applications and networks, as well as an internship program in these areas," Hass says. "We target displaced and disabled workers needing retraining, along with junior high and high schools that want to develop work programs for their students in computer repair and network administration."

Another of the center's ideas tackles crime. At a 1995 guns-for-computers swap, hundreds of sawed-off shotguns, handguns, and other firearms were turned in for used computers on a one-to-one basis. Because of the idea's initial success, more swaps are planned. Another idea involves opening up "street schools" in empty storefronts by lining up used computers for anyone to use and learn on. "With the help of volunteers at these street schools," Hass explains, "anyone will be able to walk in and learn how to use computers to either boost job skills or simply self-esteem."

## For More Information

*Write to the Computer Recycling Center, 1245 Terra Bella Avenue, Mountain View, CA 94043, or call (415) 428–3700.*

# Turning Old Circuit Boards into New Products

In another computer-recycling effort, industrial waste is helping to broaden the art world. When a New York City art restorer came across a bunch of circuit boards that had been removed from old computers, he didn't see trash. Instead, he saw art. As a result, he started a company called Tecnotes that reclaims defective or obsolete boards and turns them into a number of unique products.

Circuit boards are a vital component of nearly every modern electronic product. They are strong plastic sheets, stamped with detailed copper mazes and a series of holes where transistors are usually placed. The boards fit inside electronic devices to help direct their actions. Tecnotes, located in Sag Harbor, New York, pays a fee to circuit-board producers, who reject 3 to 5 percent of all the boards they produce because of defects. Tecnotes gives the rejected circuit boards new life by turning them into long-lasting three-ring binders, address books, clipboards, notebooks, and memo books. Tecnotes also produces clocks, coasters, and key rings from the boards and is developing still more unusual products. The company has converted more than 150 tons of circuit boards into resourceful objects of art. They also serve as everyday items with a futuristic look.

"It's a difficult process to get rid of the waste created by these boards," says Mitch Davis, Tecnotes' president. "It's not economical to melt them down, and it's expensive to haul them to landfills—not to mention the negative environmental effects

*This Tecnote clock was made from an ordinary computer circuit board.*

of both alternatives. Instead, we produce durable products out of material that would otherwise be headed for the trash.

"Getting a second use from these items and creating useful products while using little energy is what we're all about. We've taken recycling a step further by re-using the material as it is—without any reprocessing."

Tecnotes products are sold in more than a dozen countries, and sales continue to grow. Many of the products have been featured in museum exhibits displaying forms of art using computer or recycling themes, including a show at the Museum of Modern Art in New York City. Because circuit-board designs vary greatly, each product has a unique look. Most of the boards have a green background and are covered with varying patterns of copper lines that make them look like futuristic city maps. The binders are held together with hinges made from recycled plastic. "Everyone feels good about recycling," Davis says. "Our products simply let them re-use something at the same time."

*Tecnotes products, such as these clipboards and key chains, are sold all over the world.*

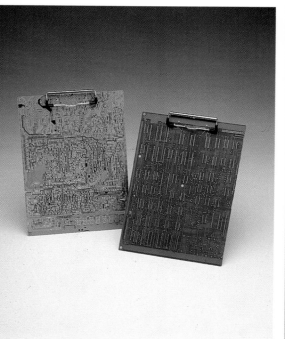

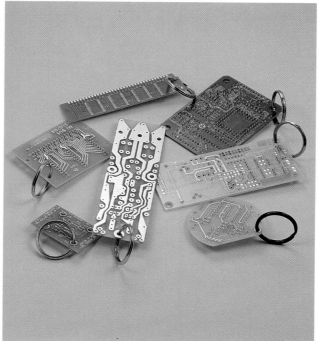

## For More Information

*Write to Tecnotes, P.O. Box 3140, Sag Harbor, NY 11963, or call (800) 331–2006. You can visit its home page at http://www.mps.org/~tecnotes/*

# Eco Disks Are Making a Difference

In Texas, a different kind of company is re-using yet another type of computer product. Each year, an estimated 1 billion computer disks are purchased in the United States. Stacked on top of each other, they would form a pile more than 2,000 miles high! Surprisingly, millions more of these disks never even touch consumers' hands before heading for a landfill. This most often happens when a software company upgrades one of its products—going from say, version 3.1 to 3.2. At that point, thousands or even millions of unused computer disks are suddenly rendered obsolete.

In the past, these diskettes landed in the nearest landfill. Now a unique new company is taking the disks and giving them a second life through an innovative recycling idea. Eco Tech purchases disks that contain obsolete versions of software and creates blank disks, called Eco Disks, ready for use.

A friend of one of Eco Tech's original founders encountered the disk-trash problem firsthand while working for a computer company. He watched as truckload after truckload of outdated software disks were carted off to a landfill; the cost to reclaim the disks by removing the useless adhesive labels and erasing the old software programs on them was too high to justify doing in-house recycling. Then, one night at a kitchen table, Eco Tech's founders thought of a way to remove the old stick-on labels—the main obstacle to recycling them. Through trial and error, they eventually developed a machine to handle the task. The company now contracts with major software and computer manufacturers to obtain 3.5-inch disks loaded with old software.

When Eco Tech receives packages of software, all manuals and cardboard boxes are first separated out for recycling. The diskettes are then sorted into categories, such as high density or double density. Next, the disks are erased using an elecromagnetic device that eliminates all data as well as any computer viruses. Twisted or damaged disks are broken down into parts, which are eventually recycled. The labels of the remaining disks are removed through a patented process that uses no chemicals. Then the disks are formatted for use in either IBM-based or Macintosh computers and packaged for resale in recycled paper boxes.

Each disk carries a lifetime warranty, and new labels, printed on recycled paper with vegetable ink, are provided. Because the original software manufacturers use only the highest-quality materials, the disks are superior to many other versions on the market. In addition, they have been programmed or written on only once, which gives them great value. The products are indistinguishable from any other blank disks used to store computer-generated information.

For a service fee, Eco Tech also provides recycling services by taking existing disks, reformatting and delabeling them, and then returning them to companies. Interested companies can also send Eco Tech their obsolete disks and receive a rebate of 20 percent of the total disks reclaimed.

"The company has now processed upwards of 500,000 disks and handles about 40,000 a month," General Manager Rick Wynn explains. "Before, they were just thrown in the trash by the millions—and they are there forever. We're simply repackaging something that hasn't even been used before."

### For More Information
*Write to Eco Tech, 11450 F.M. 1960 West, Suite 208, Houston, TX 77065, or call (800) ECO–6175.*

# Recycled Materials in the Fashion World

Due to recent worldwide interest in recycling technologies, designers and businesspeople in the clothing and fashion industries have found that recycled materials actually make functional and highly desirable clothing. People seem to enjoy buying and wearing recycled clothes and other items. As a result of this trend, plastic soda pop bottles, inner tubes, and other forms of garbage are finding new lives as dresses, purses, and backpacks. The trend saves natural resources and landfill space. It's also making money for some creative businesses.

## Recycled Cotton Makes Better Clothing

The process of turning cotton into various products causes numerous problems for the environment. In the manufacturing of cotton fabrics, millions of cotton fibers fly off during the spinning process and fall to the floor. Typically, these fibers—called mill trimmings—are swept up and carted off to a landfill.

A New Jersey company, however, is now collecting these fibers and using them to make a line of recycled-cotton socks, T-shirts, and baseball caps. Founded in 1992, Take the Lead, Inc., makers of Better World® clothing, has already sold more than 250,000 pairs of their recycled-cotton socks, along with more than 500,000 pairs of another line of socks made from organically grown cotton.

Take the Lead, Inc., is the United States' only recycled-cotton sock maker in the mainstream market. The company receives mill trimmings from clothing manufacturers in North Carolina, South Carolina, and Tennessee. Take the Lead's yarn-spinning mills then clean the trimmings and re-spin them with virgin cotton to gain the correct length of cotton fibers needed to make Better World® socks. The final mixture is 75 percent recycled cotton to 25 percent virgin (previously unused) cotton. The company continues to re-use trimmings that it generates.

"In using recycled cotton, we're saving landfill space by re-using a good material instead of wasting it—and we're encouraging recycling efforts by reinforcing the notion that everything can be re-used again for another purpose," Loraine Kulik, director of community partnerships, explains. "It hasn't

*Scraps of recycled cotton are turned into new cotton clothing such as these T-shirts and socks.*

always been easy, though. We have had to spend a great deal of time encouraging, inspiring, and convincing manufacturers to use both organic cotton and recycled cotton to make Better World® products."

*Take the Lead co-founders Dominic Careri Kulik and David Yaskulka stand with Ben Cohen and Jerry Greenfield of Ben & Jerry's Homemade Ice Cream. Ben & Jerry helped inspire them to start their for-profit business.*

Five years ago, the co-founders of Take the Lead started a nonprofit organization called LEAD, which is an acronym for Leadership, Education, and Development. The program involves college students who work together on environmental and social issues in their local neighborhoods. The students design and teach courses to younger students on these issues and receive school credit for their efforts.

"But eventually the co-founders wanted to also create a 'for-profit' business to try and close the gap between business, family, and environmental issues," Kulik says. "One of the co-founders' fathers—who had spent 15 years in the sock business—joined the effort. So socks it was."

Better World® socks can be found in more than 30 of the nation's department-store chains, including Nordstrom's, May Company, Dayton-Hudson's, and Dillard's. They are also on the shelves of more than 300 college and university bookstores as well as numerous environmental shops. The company currently produces 17 women's cotton-sock styles and six men's styles.

### For More Information

*Write to Take the Lead, Inc., 2010 Center Avenue, Suite 1, Fort Lee, NJ 07024, or call (800) 532–3411.*

# From Pop Bottles to Clothing

Along with recycled cotton fibers, recycled plastic has also expanded into the multimillion-dollar world of fashion, and this is good news for the environment. Wellman, Inc., one of the world's largest fiber producers, is also the world's largest and most advanced recycler of plastic. Its polyester, for instance, is marketed under the Fortrel® brand name. In 1993, the company launched Fortrel® EcoSpun—a revolutionary fiber made from 100 percent recycled plastic (PET) from soda, water, and food containers.

"What makes EcoSpun such an exciting breakthrough is that it gives consumers many more options to close the loop in PET recycling," says Jim Casey, president of Wellman's fiber division. "EcoSpun's success is proof that it can be fashionable to be environmentally proactive."

In its introductory period, the recycled fabric was predominantly used for outdoor apparel. Wellman's ongoing research and development, however, led to broader applications, including golf shirts, socks, sweaters, backpacks, and luggage. "For every pound of 100 percent EcoSpun, approximately ten PET bottles are kept out of America's landfills," Casey explains. "We reclaim up to 2.4 billion bottles every year."

Companies like Patagonia, L.L. Bean, and Land's End have already featured EcoSpun products in their clothing lines. Nordstrom's, Saks, Macy's, and J.C. Penney have also distributed various products made from the material. Wellman has been so successful with EcoSpun that the company is already

Fortrel® EcoSpun fiber is made from 100 percent recycled plastic containers.

operating at full capacity. "When we started in April 1993, we had only one manufacturer using the fabric. Now, well over 200 manufacturers are using EcoSpun in everything from thermal underwear to eco-denim in jeans," Casey boasts.

Wellman began business in 1927. The company started making nylon and polyester fibers from recycled raw materials in the mid-1960s at its Johnsonville, South Carolina, plant. In 1972, Wellman International began operations in Ireland to produce similar polyester and nylon fibers for various European markets. To this day, the Irish plant and Wellman's two

South Carolina plants produce nothing but materials made of 100 percent recycled plastic. And as a whole, 40 percent of the company's total fiber production comes from recycled materials.

The company received a fashion-industry award for environmental excellence from the United Nations' Environmental Program in 1993. The company also received the president's award for sustainable development at the White House, an Edison Innovation Award from the American Marketing Association, and the 1994 Keep America Beautiful National Award.

Because EcoSpun is made from containers that were primarily used for food, these bottles are made of exceptionally high-quality plastic. When cleaned, melted down, and drawn out, they produce an excellent fiber. When the EcoSpun fiber is spun into yarn and knitted and woven into fabrics, the results are extremely versatile—making everything from velvet upholstery and linenlike cloth to thick pile material for jackets and protective outer layers for soft-side luggage. The high-grade polyester fiber has all the properties of virgin polyester.

"EcoSpun is strong, washable, dryable, and holds color," Casey says. "Right now, you won't find a real silky blouse made of EcoSpun, but we're working on it. We're trying to make it even finer, which will make the fiber even more versatile." Apparel and home furnishings can all be made from EcoSpun, and future applications seem limitless. "Every day, fashion professionals make thousands of decisions that have an impact on this fragile planet," says Casey. "Ecospun is a new fiber that can help them conserve the world's resources, whether as 100 percent polyester or in blends with cotton, wool, spandex, nylon, and other fibers."

In 1992 alone, Wellman recycled 100 million pounds of plastic beverage bottles—the fuel-oil content of which could power a city the size of Atlanta, Georgia, for one year. "Unfortunately, there's a bottle shortage," explains Casey. "The price of recycled bottles has doubled in the last year. Future growth in this area is dependent on a national bottle-recycling law. Right now, only eight states have mandatory recycling

*These kids are wearing "green" tops and shorts made with EcoSpun.*

laws for PET bottles, and there hasn't been a new one since 1985."

Despite the shortage, PET bottles already represent a recycling success story. In 1995, 34 percent of all PET bottles in the United States were recycled, versus just 3 percent of all plastic. "Wellman is closing the loop by giving people back a Patagonia jacket or a backpack—that's magic," Casey says with a smile. By recycling PET, the world's landfill space is spared, our planet's natural resources are preserved, and air and water pollution are lessened.

## For More Information

*Write to Wellman, Inc., 1133 Avenue of the Americas, New York, NY 10036, or call (212) 642–0793.*

# Recycled Rubber Serves Its Purpose

As millions of tires and inner tubes continue to sit in dumps and landfills around North America, one person is trying to make a dent in the problem—although a small one at this point. Mandana MacPherson, founder of Used Rubber USA, in San Francisco, California, produces a line of handmade and fashionable products made from used truck and bus inner tubes.

Since its beginning eight years ago, MacPherson's product line has grown to include purses, bags, belts, wallets, briefcases, notebooks, and even eyeglass cases.

The idea struck MacPherson while she was attending art school at Brown University in Rhode Island. Carrying around art supplies one day, she spilled an ink bottle and ruined a leather bag. While searching for a replacement that would resist messes caused by art supplies, she found nothing. Eventually, MacPherson came across an old inner tube and created a bag she could use to carry her art supplies. Her friends liked it, and she ended up making several more, selling them in a few stores in Boston, Massachusetts, and New York City. "This was before the

The handbags these women are carrying and the fasteners on their coats are all made from recycled rubber.

environmental movement was in full gear," MacPherson recalls. "People liked the black color, the shapes and styles, and the unusual textures in the rubber."

Unlike bags and purses made of vinyl or plastic, Used Rubber USA's bags are worth the extra cost needed to clean the rubber and create the products because they will last such a long time. In fact, the products come with a lifetime guarantee and are one of the few durable and waterproof alternatives to leather.

"It's comparable in price to leather, but lasts forever. Some people still have the perception of it as trash, but acceptance is growing," MacPherson adds. "We sell a lot of items strictly based on style. But we don't consider them a novelty—they're functional and fashionable."

*Stylish yet sturdy bags are some of the products made from re-cycled rubber.*

Because there is no system in place to handle the collection of used inner tubes, Used Rubber USA serves as both the collector and re-user of the waste product. The company works with a number of tire shops in the San Francisco area to collect the used inner tubes. It goes through more than 10 tons of used rubber a year. Each product varies slightly in markings and textures due to the different patterns found on the inner tubes. The products incorporate rustproof, all-aluminum rivets, and the rubber can be cleaned with soap and water.

*Mandana Mac-Pherson (right) uses inner tubes and tires to make her fashionable products.*

## For More Information

*Write to Used Rubber USA, 597 Haight Street, San Francisco, CA 94117, or call (415) 626–7855.*

# Alaskan Eco-Fashion

Salmon meat is enjoyed by millions of people around the world. And now a natural by-product of this fish is also being used. Does anyone want a fish-skin wallet?

Salmon skins are ordinarily discarded on the ocean floor after fisheries have taken the meat. By re-using the skins and turning them into striking leather products, an Alaskan company was able to help the environment and make a profit at the same time.

The art of tanning (preparing and preserving the skins) fish skins has been practiced by native Alaskans for centuries. But in 1991, a handful of entrepreneurs revived and refined this ancient process to create a beautiful end product.

Discarded fish skins cause disposal problems for the fishing and canning industry. "Typically, the skins are mulched and dumped onto the ocean floor," says Jerry Garner, president of the Juneau-based Alaskins Leather Company.

Unfortunately, the skins are 50 percent pure protein, composed mostly of scales. This protein does not break down, and it ends up on the ocean floor. This seemingly "organic" waste actually suffocates whatever it lands upon.

Alaskins used more than 700,000 fish skins to make its products in one year. That's more than 150,000 pounds of previously unwanted material that were put to good use.

"We are allowing for complete utilization of the species," Garner says. "And we're proud of that."

Four partners started the company together in 1987 by tinkering with a tanning process that used plastic trash cans and wooden paddles. After 18 months of effort, they produced samples of their products. They decided to sell some of their goods at a local trade show. The event was successful—the partners sold absolutely everything they brought to the show. Alaskins products include wallets, checkbook covers, boots, jewelry, and business-card holders. Former president Gerald Ford even uses a set of salmon-skin golf-club covers that were given to him in 1995 by the gover-

nor of Alaska. Alaskins fish leather was also used for costumes in the movie *Return to the Blue Lagoon.*

By the end of 1988, Alaskins products were in more than 100 Alaska stores, including every J.C. Penney outlet in the state. Alaskins produced 26 different items from three fish species—salmon, halibut, and sea bass. Alaskins is no longer in business, but its approach to recycling was unique and the effort noteworthy.

*Alaskins leather was used to create the costumes worn in* Return to the Blue Lagoon.

47

# Unique Recycling Ideas

*A*lthough most people think of recycling in terms of the most commonly used materials, like glass, paper, plastic, and aluminum, it is not limited to these items. Any idea or product that keeps materials out of landfills by giving them another life can make an important difference in the well-being of the environment. Clever and innovative approaches to recycling are being developed every day as people begin to understand the many values of recycling. Some of these unique approaches are described in this chapter.

# BIOtees Designed to Biodegrade Fast

A teenage entrepreneur from Evergreen, Colorado, developed a golf tee made of recycled materials in an effort to make one aspect of the sport more "environmentally friendly."

Golf tees are small, but their impact adds up when golfers use new ones time after time. Each year, more than 1.5 billion golf tees are used in the sport—the equivalent of 35,000 mature birch trees. "I knew that if I used recycled materials, the tees would help save trees and stop those materials from going to landfills," explains Casey Golden, creator of the BIOtee.

*Casey Golden mixes up a batch of BIOtees.*

Casey won the grand prize in the Invent America contest for his invention.

The idea for this new form of golf tee came indirectly from Casey's father, who used to work as a greenskeeper and knew what broken tees could do to lawn mowers. "Whenever I went golfing with my dad, he made me pick up the broken tees," Casey recalls. "Finally I said, 'Why can't these things just go away naturally?'"

When a project at school required students to think of a problem and come up with a creative solution, Casey—then 13 years old—went to work creating a biodegradable tee—one that would decompose naturally, unlike the wooden and plastic versions used by most golfers. His original formula included flour, water, fertilizer, peat moss, and applesauce. The unusual mixture was then pressed into homemade molds and hardened in the microwave oven. Casey entered his idea in the Invent America contest, a national competition sponsored by the U.S. Commerce Department for kindergarteners through eighth graders. He won the $1,000 grand prize for his grade level.

Now patented, the BIOtee is composed of recycled paper, recycled plant fibers, water-soluble binders, and a pulplike by-product from the beverage industry. Golfers won't notice a difference when using a BIOtee to tee up their golf balls. But once one of the tees is used, broken, and left behind, it soaks up water (when it rains or when the sprinklers come on). The next mowing then disperses the material as mulch. If golfers used BIOtees exclusively, nearly 1 million pounds of waste would be diverted from landfills every year.

Casey's father, John Golden, is the president of Bio-Dynamics, Ltd., a company that the family started in order to produce and market the BIOtee. Numerous molds produce batches of the tees every 35 seconds. The round-the-clock operation produces 75,000 tees a day. Orders are rolling in. Other manufacturing alternatives are being explored.

BIOtees are now being sold in K-mart stores across the country. The company has featured Casey on the cover of one of its quarterly reports, honoring both his entrepreneurial skills and his environmental awareness. "It's been interesting," Casey says of the path that his idea has taken. "You'd think it would be easy to just make golf tees, but it takes a lot more effort than I first thought."

*BIOtees have been patented and are purchased by golfers all over the country.*

### For More Information

*Write to Bio-Dynamics, P.O. Box 2013, Evergreen, CO 80437-2013, or call (303) 681–3305.*

## RePlay Kits Promote Environmental Fun

Playing with garbage doesn't sound like much fun, but that is exactly the idea behind RePlay Activity Kits for children. It's clean garbage that stirs kids' imaginations. The idea combines environmental education with a number of different reclaimed materials to create fun activities for children.

All of the materials included in the RePlay Activity Kits, produced by Pappa Geppetto's Toys, based in Victoria, British Columbia, Canada, are either factory scraps or business leftovers gathered from various manufacturers and companies. Non-toxic items such as beads, rubber washers, film spools, colorful paper, foil scraps, wood, and foam rubber are then transformed into all kinds of unique sculptures by children. Glue and peel-and-stick tape are included in every kit, along with some simple instructions. Kids use the items to create cars, rockets, monsters, crowns, puppets, animals, hats—anything they can think of.

"The beauty of the RePlay kits is that the contents are always changing, and new contents mean new ideas," explains Pam Grossi, vice-president of Pappa Geppetto's Toys. "And everything included has been diverted from landfills. We educate manufacturers as far as what types of items we need, and they then set up barrels to collect them for us."

Imagination Market, a nonprofit arts and recycling organization, originally developed the RePlay idea. The group collects and recycles discarded materials and conducts workshops for educators and children in the Pacific Northwest.

*RePlay kits let children create unique things, such as this mask, from recycled materials.*

*All of the contents in these RePlay Activity Kits are made from recycled materials.*

After Pappa Geppetto's crossed paths with the nonprofit group during a search for soon-to-be-discarded beads, a joint venture eventually followed. Geppetto's has been selling the activity sets in toy, environmental, nature, and museum stores for several years, as well as through a number of different catalogs.

RePlay currently has 15 different kits, each with its own theme such as hats, bike decorations, wind gizmos, jewelry, and disguises. The kits are appropriate for kids five years of age and up.

"By combining a diverse variety of unique and exciting reclaimed materials with a child's natural 'no-holds-barred' imagination, the kits encourage boundless artistic exploration and creativity," Grossi notes.

Working with materials that would otherwise be tossed in the trash also appeals to children. And because creations can be made and torn apart time after time, this is a toy that they can't break.

## For More Information
*Write to Pappa Geppetto's Toys, P.O. Box 3567, Blaine, WA 98231-3567, or call (800) 667-5407.*

# Recycling Steel Is Helpful to the Environment

After nearly 200 years of being in use, steel cans are still used for more than 90 percent of all the metal food containers sold in the United States. Recycling these millions of cans can provide an obvious benefit to landfills everywhere, and it can produce many other exciting environmental benefits. The Steel Recycling Institute (SRI), based in Pittsburgh, Pennsylvania, wants to make that happen.

"It's more economical to re-use metals than to mine them," says Bill Heenan, SRI's president. "The steel industry built recycling into its manufacturing process long ago because it was the economical thing to do during World War II, when steel supplies were short. Today, it's still the economical thing to do, but it's good for the environment, too."

According to Heenan, for each ton of steel recycled, 2,500 pounds of iron ore, 1,000 pounds of coal, and 40 pounds of limestone are saved. And recycling steel saves 75 percent of the energy required to produce the material from previously unused supplies. Each year, the industry saves the equivalent energy needed to power one fifth of the households in the United States.

SRI was founded in 1988 to promote and sustain steel recycling. Though it is based in Pittsburgh, SRI also operates seven regional offices. SRI's scope initially centered on steel cans but has since been expanded to include used appliances, cars, and construction materials.

"In 1988, about 15 percent of steel cans were recycled in this country," Heenan explains. "Today, steel cans are being recycled in virtually every program in the country, helping the recycling rate to continue to grow."

Recycling steel food cans is easy. Simply rinse the container in leftover dishwater or in extra space in the dishwasher (to conserve another precious resource, water). Empty steel food, beverage, paint, and aerosol cans are all recyclable. However, check with your community to see which are accepted in your local program and how they are collected.

Since the steel industry requires old steel in order to produce new steel, the metal can be recycled over and over again into new products. Fortunately, the industry has already established a system of steel recyclers. You might call them junk-yard

*With an enormous magnet, steel is collected for processing at a scrap yard.*

operators, but they are really scrap processors whose job it is to remove the steel from old automobiles, appliances, and other products for recycling.

*Steel containing 28 percent recycled steel moves along a conveyor at a mill.*

Steel's magnetic quality is one added bonus to recycling efforts. By sweeping a strong magnet over recyclables or mixed waste, steel cans can be easily separated from other materials. Magnets also make it easy for scrap processors to separate steel components.

"Since you can't make steel without old steel, there simply is no reason for any steel product to ever end up in a landfill," Heenan concludes.

## For More Information

*For the nearest location where you can recycle steel cans, write to the Steel Recycling Institute, 680 Andersen Drive, Pittsburgh, PA 15220-2700, or call (800) 937-1226, extension 140.*

The annual Rose Bowl Parade always starts in Pasadena, California, but until 1994, the beautiful floats always ended up at a local landfill once the parade was over. Then, thanks to a creative effort, many of the flowers from the 1994 floats ended up in thousands of homes instead.

These flowers were recycled into Genuine Tournament of Roses Potpourri.

"The potpourri keeps thousands of flowers from being thrown away, and it will benefit thousands of deserving kids," says Terri Rukenbrod, director of corporate development for the Children's Miracle Network (CMN). "We feel that it's an excellent recycling program."

CMN was started in 1983 by the Osmond family—a well-known family of entertainers. Based in Salt Lake City, Utah, the organization helps fund 166 children's hospitals and pediatric wards in Canada and the United States. More than 5 million children are helped each year. CMN helps these hospitals pay for research, new equipment, and patient services.

With the help of Florists' Transworld Delivery Association (FTD), FedEx, and the Tournament of Roses Association, CMN tested the aromatic product on a limited basis in 1993. Just nine floats produced 7,000 bags of potpourri, which were quickly sold. In 1994, all 56 floats were used to produce about 50,000 bags of potpourri.

After the parade, about 200 volunteers, including schoolchildren and retirees, picked the flowers off the floats. FedEx

shipped the flowers to Florida for freeze-drying and then to Arkansas for packaging. It was FTD, however, that came up with the original idea.

"Since the roses were traditionally tossed out after the Rose Bowl Parade, we thought that it was a unique recycling idea that could help a very worthy cause," says Richard Williams, FTD's assistant director of consumer communications. "The potpourri serves as an example of the importance and success of recycling."

The sales of the potpourri generated around $250,000 for CMN. In addition to providing the fund-raising idea, FTD coordinated most of the sales and deliveries for CMN. The product also was sold in many hospital gift shops. FTD has since dropped its sponsorship of the program, but the Tournament of Roses Committee is looking for new partners to keep the unique recycling project alive.

*The flowers used on floats, such as this one, were turned into potpourri in a unique recycling effort.*

# Recycling Facts

- The United States generates 157 million tons of garbage per year, or 432,000 tons of garbage every day.
- Enough energy is saved by recycling one can to power a television for three hours.
- Each year, recycling saves enough energy to supply Los Angeles, California, with electricity for nearly a decade.
- Making one ton of recycled paper uses only about 60 percent of the energy consumed by making one ton of virgin paper.
- Today, there are about 7,265 curbside recycling programs in the United States serving 108 million people. There were only 3,900 programs in 1991.
- More than 240 million tires are discarded annually in the United States.
- Approximately 2.7 million tons of aluminum waste is generated annually in the United States, and 54 percent of it is recycled.
- Steel makes up about 6 percent of the waste stream in America, with approximately 12.3 million tons generated each year. About 41 percent is recycled, and 53 percent of steel cans are recycled.
- In 1993, a total of 56 percent, or 6.4 million tons, of old newspapers were recycled.
- Americans throw away enough plastic soda bottles in a year to circle the planet four times. A third of them are recycled.
- Plastic comprises 20 percent of the material sent to landfills. An average American consumes 220 pounds of plastic each year, mostly in product packaging. In Latin America, each person accounts for only 22 pounds of plastic each year.
- About 13.2 million tons of glass are disposed of annually in the United States, composing 6.7 percent of the waste stream. Approximately 20 percent is recycled.
- Before you or your parents buy a product, consider how you will dispose of it and its packaging—"precycling."
- The world's largest landfill is on Staten Island, New York.

# Glossary

**acronym** When the intitial letters of a phrase or long name spell another word that can be substituted as an abbreviation; for example, POP (Plastic On Parks).

**biodegradable** Something that decomposes naturally.

**charitable** Something related to a charity or nonprofit organization.

**entrepreneur** A person who spends time and or money pursuing business opportunities for himself or herself.

**formaldehyde** A colorless gas used as a disinfectant, preservative, and for making other compounds.

**groundwater** Water that has flowed or seeped beneath the surface of the earth. It is the source of water for underground springs and wells.

**insulation** Something used to resist the transfer of heat, cold, or electrical current.

**landfill** Trash disposal that involves burying garbage in the ground; a landfill is often a huge pit in the ground.

**nonprofit** A group or organization that pursues activities without direct financial benefit to owners or stockholders.

**obsolete** Something that has become useless because of technological or lifestyle changes.

**organic** Something grown from, or a by-product of, a tree, plant, or animal; something grown without exposure to humanmade chemicals.

**patent** Something protected by a trademark or trade name.

**porous** Something with pores, or holes, of various sizes.

**potpourri** A fragrant mixture of dried flower petals.

**pulp** Any soft, moist, formless mass, such as a mixture of water and ground wood fibers used in making paper.

**resin** Sticky plant excretions that are often used to improve plastics and paints.

**rivet** A pin or bolt used to fasten two pieces together.

**simulate** To imitate the action or appearance of something.

**tanning**  The process of preserving and preparing hides or skins to convert them to leather.

**test market**  A test of the sales potential of a new product or service.

**texture**  The feel, or grain, of an object.

**ton**  A measurement: 2,000 pounds of weight.

**topographical map**  A map that reflects changes in elevation with a series of tightly woven and contoured lines.

**transistor**  An electronic device used to control electric current.

**virgin material**  A raw material that has never been used by humans before.

**vocational**  Related to training for a skill or trade.

# *Further Reading*

Blashfield, Jean F., and Black, Wallace B. *Recycling.* Danbury, CT: Children's Press, 1991.

Foster, Joanne. *Cartons, Cans, and Orange Peels: Where Does Our Garbage Go?* Boston, MA: Clarion, 1991.

Gay, Kathlyn. *Garbage and Recycling.* Springfield, NJ: Enslow, 1991.

Gutnik, Martin J. *Recycling: Learning the Four R's: Reduce, Reuse, Recycle, Recover.* Springfield, NJ: Enslow, 1993.

James, Barbara. *Waste and Recycling.* Chatham, NJ: Raintree Steck-Vaughn, 1990.

Stwertka, Eve, and Stwertka, Albert. *Cleaning Up: How Trash Becomes Treasure.* Morristown, NJ: Silver Burdett, 1993.

# Index

## Photo Credits

Cover: Photodisc; page 8: Chicago Parks, Landscape Management, and Recreation Departments; page 9: Plastic Recycling, Inc.; page 11: Recycled Plastic Products, Inc.; page 16: Forest Saver/Steve Lindner; pages 18, 19: Phenix Biocomposites; page 21: ©Michael P. Gadomski/Photo Researchers, Inc.; page 22: Courtesy Paper Services Limited/Greg Bolosky; page 24: Woods End Research Laboratory, Inc.; page 27: ©Porter Gifford/Gamma Liaison; page 28: ©Russell D. Curtis/Photo Researchers, Inc.; pages 31, 32: Tecnotes; pages 37, 38: Better World®; page 40: ©Aaron Strong/Liaison International; page 42: ©Larry Prosor; pages 43, 44, 45: Photos by Mandana MacPherson; page 47: Photofest; pages 49, 50, 51: ©Shock Photography; pages 53, 54: Pappa Geppetto's Toys; pages 56, 57: Steel Recycling Institute; page 59: ©Lawrence Migdale/Photo Researchers, Inc.